THE GOODNESS OF
PEPPERS
· · · · · · · · · · ·

JOHN MIDGLEY

Illustrated by

IAN SIDAWAY

RANDOM HOUSE
NEW YORK

ACKNOWLEDGEMENTS

The author thanks Sue Midgley and Jo Swinnerton
for kindly checking the text, and Susan Bell of Random House
for suggesting the subject of peppers for the series.

FURTHER READING

Amal Naj's excellent book, *Peppers: A Story of Hot Pursuits*
(Knopf, 1992) is a lively read.
For those interested in reading more about food and health
The Food Pharmacy, by Jean Carper (Simon and Schuster)
and *Superfoods* by Michael Van Straten and
Barbara Griggs (Dorling Kindersley) are recommended.
Reay Tannahill's *Food in History* (Penguin) is recommended
to all with an interest in the history of food.

Published in the United States by Random House, Inc., New York.

This work was published in Great Britain by
Pavilion Books Limited, London.

ISBN 0-679-42680-9

Library of Congress Cataloging-in-Publication Data is available.

Manufactured in Hong Kong

2 4 6 8 9 7 5 3

First U.S. Edition

CONTENTS

. . . .

PART ONE

THE GENUS *CAPSICUM*

....

C ultivated sweet peppers and several kinds of cultivated chillies such as the jalapeño are the fruits of
Capsicum annuum, an annual plant that is native to
northern South America though cultivated in many different parts of the world. *Capsicum annuum* is the largest
species. *Capsicum frutescens*, its very close relative, is a
perennial plant that almost certainly derives from the
same ancestral plant as *Capsicum annuum*, and grows
wild in tropical America. Many of the smaller, cultivated chillies, such as the tabasco pepper, and several
wild varieties belong to *Capsicum frutescens*. Other recognized species are *Capsicum chinense*, to which the
explosively hot habanero and bonnet peppers belong;
Capsicum pubescens, the parent of the Andean rocoto
pepper; and *Capsicum baccatum*. All capsicum species
belong to the Solanaceae family and are related to potatoes, tomatoes, aubergines (eggplants), tobacco and
nightshade.

Sweet peppers and chillies alike start off green,
ripening to yellow and finally to red, although some
varieties of peppers are cultivated specifically for their
more unusual colours, ranging from purplish-black to
lilac and cream. Peppers picked while still green will
not ripen and change colour; they do so only while the
fruit is still attached to the plant.

Nomenclature is very variable and confused. For
many, peppers is an all-embracing term for sweet and
hot capsicums, while for others only mild, sweet capsicums count as peppers, and the rest are chillies. The
terms 'bell' and 'sweet' pepper are often applied to any
kind of large, mild, fleshy pepper. (The former is preferred in the United States, while in Britain the latter
predominates.) 'Pimiento' is used in different contexts,
whether as the Spanish name for sweet red peppers, or
more specifically to describe red peppers that have
been skinned and filleted, or even preserved in oil or

pickled in vinegar. In fact, the pimiento is a sweet variety originally planted in Spain that resembles the common bell pepper, but with a more tapering base that lacks the characteristic lobes of the bell pepper.

In Britain, chillies are rarely classified according to any criteria other than their size (large, medium and small), heat (hot or mild), colour (red, yellow, orange or green), and provenance (Kenyan, Indian, Thai, etc.) By contrast, in the Americas, peppers are usually distinguished by their variety, of which a very large number is routinely available, although nomenclature is imprecise.

Some peppers have different names when sold in their fresh and dried forms; ancho peppers are dried poblanos; the fresh form of the pasilla pepper is the chilaca; chipotles sold dried, smoked or canned are none other than the very popular jalapeño, which is available fresh and pickled.

Others are much more likely to be available dried than fresh, such as the chile de árbol, Thai bird's eye chillies, and some sweet peppers, such as the squat Spanish ñora, and guindillas.

The sizes and shapes of capsicums vary enormously, from long and tapering, and squat and tapering, to pea-, cherry- and bell-shaped, with or without lobes. Among the longest is an Asian chilli measuring up to 22cm/9 inches that is as mild as the American Anaheim, and the bulkiest is probably New Mexico's 'Big Jim', resembling a small banana. Some of the smallest are round chaco chillies, and elongated bird's eye and piquín chillies.

Dried chillies are also available crumbled or flaked. Cayenne pepper (named after the capital of French Guyana) is made by drying and grinding the fruits of a hot variety of capsicum into powder, whereas chilli powder is two quite different products on either side of the Atlantic. In Britain, chilli powder simply refers to dried, ground chillies, whereas in the United

States it is the name of a darker coloured spice mixture that includes chillies as well as cumin and oregano, and is commonly used to season chilli con carne. Paprika is no less varied, and comes in varying degrees of heat. The best, Hungarian 'noble rose', is brilliantly coloured and superbly flavoured; other types of paprika are made from various European varieties of dried sweet peppers.

There are many different chilli sauces and chilli-based flavourings to be found in different parts of the world, such as Chinese, Malaysian and Caribbean chilli sauces; Louisiana hot pepper sauces, notably Tabasco®, the famous bottled sauce made by McIlhenny's in Avery Island only from salt, vinegar and juicy red pods of the eponymous pepper; North African harissa; Chinese, Thai and Malay chilli oils; soy bean and chilli pastes; Indonesian sambals; and Korean kimchi, to list but a few. Where the climate is suitably warm for peppers and chillies to be harvested in abundance, pickling and sun-drying are the favoured methods of preservation, especially in the Mediterranean, the Balkans, Mexico, and many parts of Asia.

As a general rule (with many exceptions), the larger the pepper, the milder it will be. Thus, tiny bird's eye and tepín chillies are among the most explosively hot, while large, fleshy Anaheims are among the mildest. Flavour and aroma are also extremely varied, and the qualities are not related to a pepper's heat. For example, the habanero (named after Cuba's capital) is the hottest pepper known as well as one of the most aromatic and highly flavoured, whereas some other very hot chillies, though acrid, taste bland. No other culture has learned to exploit the nuances of bite and flavour in quite the same way as Mexico's, routinely combining several different fresh, dried and ground peppers in the same dish, although cooks in central and southern India have also developed some of that versatility.

Some fresh capsicums

Ají pepper
Amatista pepper
Anaheim chilli
Bell pepper
'Big Jim'
Bird's eye chilli
Bombay cherry pepper
Bonnet pepper
Cayenne chilli
Chaco pepper
Cherry pepper
Chilaca chilli
Chile de árbol
Chile largo
Corno di toro pepper
Cubanelle pepper
Española chilli
Fresno pepper
Guajillo chilli
Habanero pepper
Hungarian cherry pepper
Hungarian pimiento
Jalapeño chilli
Kenyan chilli
Korean chilli
Kumataka chilli
Lombok chilli
Malagueta pepper
New Mexican chillies
(*NuMex*)
Paprika pepper
Pimiento
Piquín chilli
Poblano chilli
Rajiao chilli
Rocotillo chilli

Rocoto pepper
Sandía chilli
Santaka chilli
Serrano chilli
Sweet peppers
(*red, yellow, orange, green,
white, purple, and lilac*)
Tabasco pepper
Tepín chilli
Thai chillies
Ulupica pepper
Wax pepper

Some dried capsicums

Ají pepper
Ancho chilli
Bird's eye chilli
Butter chilli
Cascabel chilli
Cayenne pepper
Chile de árbol
Chipotle chilli
Guajillo chilli
Guindilla pepper
Lombok chilli
Mulato chilli
Ñora pepper
New Mexico chillies
(*NuMex*)
Paprika pepper
Pasilla chilli
Peperoncino chillies
Piquín chilli
Serrano chilli
Tepín chilli

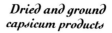

Dried and ground capsicum products

Cayenne
Chilli powder
Flaked chillies
(*hot pepper flakes*)
Paprika

Other capsicum products

Canned pimiento
Chilli bean sauce
Chilli oil
(*Chinese, Thai, Malay, etc.*)
Chilli paste
Chilli purée
Chilli relish
Chilli vinegar
Chinese chilli sauce
Curry paste ('red', 'green')
Hot Indian chutney, and pickle
Hot pepper sauce
Nam prik (chilli paste)
Preserved peppers and chillies
Sambal
Szechuan chilli paste
Tabasco® sauce

Growing peppers

C apsicums thrive in hot, tropical and sub-tropical climates. They are commonly grown domestically throughout the warmer parts of the world, in patios and back yards, on balconies and kitchen window sills and in garden plots, and the ripe fruits are harvested in summer and hung out to dry in the sun in vivid scarlet garlands or bunches.

They can also be grown successfully in temperate areas, as long as they are protected from frosts and given a position in full sun. Seeds sown in pots under glass in the spring are thinned when they become seedlings, leaving one or two healthy plants to a pot. The plants need a liquid feed every fortnight or so, once the flowers have set, and can remain in pots, or be transplanted outdoors in well-sheltered, sunny positions, or, more commonly, planted in the greenhouse and watered regularly. The growing tips should be pinched out and the fruits picked as soon as they have matured, to encourage more growth and further fruiting. They should be ready for harvesting in July if grown in a greenhouse, and in August and September if grown outdoors. (Commercially-grown peppers and chillies are available throughout the year.) Capsicums also make attractive house plants and some ornamental varieties of chilli are sold potted for this purpose.

Pepper consumption

Over a quarter of the world's population are regular pepper eaters. The greatest chilli eaters of all are the Thais, Mexicans and Indians, followed closely by the Koreans, Malays and Indonesians. The people of Szechuan, in western China, as well as many West Indians, North and West Africans and the citizens of several Central and South American countries are also great devotees. The leading growing and exporting nation of chillies is India, whose own citizens consume 95% of their crop, while that with the greatest number of different varieties is Mexico, arguably the home of the chilli pepper.

Peppers are big business in the United States. Predictably, the south and south west are home to the greatest number of chilli farms and canneries, especially the states of New Mexico, Arizona, California, Texas and Louisiana.

Sweet peppers are especially valued in the warmer European countries, most notably Italy, Spain and France (especially in their Basque regions), and throughout the Balkans and the Middle East. All these countries are major growers and exporters, as is Holland, the major exporter to Britain. Naturally, Hungary is the leading producer of paprika, followed by Spain, Portugal, Morocco, Greece and Italy, among others. Cayenne is produced in many different countries, including India, China and Mexico, but no longer in French Guyana.

Capsaicin is the flavourless substance that makes peppers hot. It is most highly concentrated in the seeds, in the inner walls towards the cap end of the pod, and in and near the pithy ribs that run along its length. The compounds that determine flavour are concentrated towards the outer walls of the pod. Consequently, even very hot chillies can be delicately but selectively chewed without drastic ill effect if the right parts of the pod are bitten. Some hot peppers are immediately searing, but the heat fades rapidly, leaving a pleasant and addictive tingling sensation in the mouth, while others are less explosive initially, but their acrid heat lingers. Sweet peppers contain very little or no capsaicin, which increases in concentration through the range of chillies, culminating among others in the tabasco, cayenne, bird's eye, piquín and, ultimately, bonnet and habanero peppers. Belonging to a broad middle range are a very large number of peppers, from the very mild, fleshy Anaheim to the famously hot jalapeño, of which a tamer variety is also cultivated for the mass market.

Peppers are notoriously variable in strength, however. Factors such as climate and soil influence their heat, so that even pods of the same variety may vary considerably, according to their provenance. Generally, the hotter the climate, the hotter the pepper. Furthermore, it is not the amount of capsaicin that determines the heat, but its chemical make-up. To introduce a universal scale to measure heat, the pharmacist Wilbur Scoville invented Scoville units. These refer to the volume of sweetened water needed to dilute capsaicin extract to the point at which virtually all traces of heat disappear when tasted on the tongue. To measure a pepper's Scoville units, first it is soaked for a few hours in a measure of alcohol into which the capsaicin leaches. This extract is then diluted in sweetened water until the heat is no longer discernible. So, to take two extremes, it takes between 200,000 and 350,000 times the volume of water to a habanero's capsaicin extract to remove all discernible heat, and only 250 to 1,400 times the volume when Anaheim peppers are subjected to the same test. Now a state-of-the-art computerized test known as HPLC (High Pressure Liquid Chromatograph) is used alongside Scoville's method of heat testing.

Buying and handling peppers

When buying fresh peppers, always reject limp, shrivelled, or soft specimens, or peppers with wrinkled patches, and look for bright, firm, glossy skins, unblemished by dark spots. They will keep perfectly well in a plastic food bag for up to a week in the refrigerator. Surplus chillies can be pickled, frozen, or skinned and preserved in oil. They will also dry out in an airy or warm place, and can be reconstituted in water, or added directly to the dish, as required.

Some cooks always wear rubber gloves when seeding or otherwise handling hot peppers prior to cooking with them. Certainly, hands that have touched cut chillies should always be washed thoroughly in cold water, and even then should not touch or rub sensitive skin such as that around the eyes and nostrils. These precautions are equally valid when handling dried chillies and cayenne.

Much of the heat of chillies is neutralized by certain starchy foods such as corn, rice and bread, and by dairy products, especially cheese and yoghurt; it is no wonder that chillies are traditionally paired with these foods.

THE GOODNESS OF PEPPERS
· · · · · · · · · ·

The principal nutritional value of all peppers is their very high concentration of vitamin C. When it has ripened to a yellow, orange or red colour, the common sweet pepper contains up to four times as much vitamin C as an orange, and just one small green pepper provides more than double the recommended daily requirement. A regular intake of vitamin C is essential to health, and the vitamin is suspected of playing an important role in cancer prevention, being an antioxidant. Peppers also contain small amounts of the antioxidant vitamin E and, like all fresh vegetables, provide valuable dietary fibre, as well as iron and potassium.

Yellow and orange vegetables are also an excellent source of sulforaphane, which accelerates the natural process of detoxification in the body, helping to block the earliest pre-tumour stages of cancer by boosting the body's resistance to carcinogens. Red and yellow capsicums are also rich in beta carotene, which is converted by the body into vitamin A, also essential to health. Beta carotene is associated with disease prevention, especially of cancers affecting the lungs, larynx, oesophagus and other mucigenous organs.

Moreover, capsaicin in chillies may act as an anti-coagulant. Research has indicated that Thais and other regular chilli-eaters suffer less from blood clots than groups that shun hot peppers. In this respect, hot peppers may offer the kind of protection against cardio-vascular disease more commonly associated with olive oil and garlic.

In common with other hot ingredients such as horseradish, true pepper, mustard and certain 'hot' spices, chillies are very effective in alleviating bronchitis and sinusitis by re-activating the flow and dispersal of blocked or heavy mucous, which can become too thick and sticky for the cilia to disperse, inflaming air passages. Capsaicin triggers a flow of water to dilute the mucous which can then be dispersed normally. Recent research has given some scientific validity to ancient Chinese and Indian practice grounded in maintaining a balance of cold and heat, or 'yin' and 'yang', in the body. In traditional medicine corrective doses of 'hot' and 'cold' substances are administered when one or other is believed to be deficient; thus, 'hot' substances are used to treat patients suffering from 'cold' effects. (For the healthy, meals are composed with cooling and heating foods properly balanced.) People who joke about eating hot, spicy foods to blast away head colds are unwittingly accurate in their observation! American research has revealed that chilli-eaters, in common with other regular indulgers in hot foods, rarely suffer from chronic bronchitis and sinusitis. In short, hot foods, especially chillies, trigger expectoration just as expectorant medicines do. They are also widely believed to aid digestion, perhaps by boosting salivation on chewing and swallowing, and increasing the flow of gastric juices. While opinion is divided on the subject, it is also possible that peppers may help ulcer sufferers by stimulating a layer of protective mucous in the stomach.

Finally, capsaicin has aroused some scientific interest as an effective local anaesthetic that relieves tooth and gum ache, and pain caused by shingles, without provoking side-effects.

Other benefits to health

Ever since their introduction into Europe in the fifteenth century, peppers have been used to treat a wide range of conditions, from digestive and respiratory problems, to infertility, inflammation, arthritis, strained muscles, toothache, alcoholism, and diarrhoea. Earlier, they were widely valued medicinally by Aztec and Inca Indians. They are a common ingredient in numerous tropical folk remedies all over the world. In structure and effect, many synthesized drugs closely resemble the therapeutically active compounds in natural ingredients such as peppers, for which greater scientific recognition seems likely.

A 'pepper high' is a curious state of mild euphoria that is sometimes experienced by determined hot pepper eaters who describe a sensation of floating detachment from the rest of the body. The effect may be caused by endorphins (natural pain killers), released by the brain in response to pain signals received from the victim's burning lips and mouth.

Peppers in History
Etymology

The English word pepper and Italian *peperone* come from the Latin *piper*, via German *pfeffer*, with a possible root in *pipali*, the Sanskrit word for 'berry', or 'peppercorn'. Capsicum derives from Latin *capsa*, 'a case' although a less likely derivation might be the Greek *kapto*, 'to bite'. Chilli, and the Spanish form, *chile* are borrowed directly from the Aztec word *chilli*. The Inca word for peppers, *ají* survives in parts of Central and South America, especially Bolivia and Peru, where pods of *Capsicum baccatum* are known by that name. *Paprika* is the Magyar word for a Hungarian variety of sweet pepper, and *pimiento* is a corruption of *pimienta*, the Spanish word for true pepper.

A brief history of peppers

It is known for certain from the discovery of seeds in neolithic caves in the Tamaulipas mountains in Mexico that peppers were gathered and eaten by American Indians about eight thousand years ago. It is more difficult to determine when peppers were first cultivated, although this seems likely to have occurred around seven thousand years ago. An intact carbonized specimen identified as belonging to the species *Capsicum annuum* was found in Tehuacan with remains of squashes, gourds, avocados and corn, suggesting the domestication of these plants for food in that period. (Earlier food remnants were confined to pepper seeds and avocado pits.)

From these earliest times, peppers seem to have been valued equally as an indispensable seasoning to enliven bland staple ingredients, and as a vegetable. Chillies and peppers were essential to the starchy diet of the Mexican Aztecs, the Incas of Peru, and other

Indians. The Aztecs used them in soups, porridge, stews and sauces, strewed them on corn tortillas, and puréed them with vegetables or fruit, just as Mexicans do today. When the Spaniards first introduced chocolate into Spain it was spiced with chillies, in the Aztec fashion: it was not appreciated at Court.

The main objective of Columbus's original voyage in 1492 was to find a sea route to India ahead of rival European fleets in order to dominate trade in the spices of the Indies, especially the berries of *piper nigrum*. On landing in the West Indies he mistook the Indians' hot peppers for a form of true pepper, and called them by the same Spanish name, *pimienta*, just as he mistook the people for their namesakes in the true Indies. Although slow to become popular, capsicums, rich in vitamin C, were used by Spanish sailors to ward off scurvy, and seeds were eventually widely planted in Spain where they remain favoured fresh and dried vegetables.

Meanwhile Portuguese navigators first met peppers further south, on the coast of Brazil, then carried them east, first to Africa, then to India, landing at their colony in Goa. Until then heat was provided by the native peppercorn for which an insatiable European demand motivated Columbus's journey. (It is ironic that this same demand led to the discovery of chillies which the real Indians adopted with enormous enthusiasm and which today are a major cash crop in that country.) The Portuguese also carried hot peppers to their settlements in Malacca, Macau, on the southern tip of China, and the Philippines. Chillies soon spread throughout Indochina, south east Asia and the far east, with tremendous and enduring impact. Amazingly, they reached Korea and Japan before the fifteenth century was out, eventually returning to their native America aboard Dutch and English slave ships.

The Ottoman Turks promoted peppers in Europe, acquiring them during their Indian campaign, and planting crops throughout the sixteenth and seventeenth centuries in occupied lands such as Hungary where eventually they became so popular as to become the national culinary emblem.

Early botanists could not agree on the number of species. While in 1700 de Tournefort, the French physician who first gave the genus the name *Capsicum* recognized just one species (with twenty-seven varieties), Linnaeus eventually recognized six. Other botanists later classified as many as fifty species. Pharmaceutical interest in peppers prompted Wilbur Scoville to perfect his system for classifying peppers according to their heat in 1912. Without peppers, the Hungarian scientist Szent-Györgyi would not have won his Nobel prize in 1932 for isolating ascorbic acid – vitamin C – from pepper extract.

By the 1920s, the popularity of sweet and hot peppers as food had grown sufficiently to sustain a significant horticultural trade in Europe (especially in Holland, where exotic fruit and vegetables have been grown since the sixteenth century), and in the United States, where there was increasing demand from the canning industry. It was then, at the height of the Jazz Age, that hot pepper sauces became fashionable, although Tabasco® dates back to a family recipe of 1870. Today our appetite for peppers and chillies has been stimulated further by the growing interest in healthy Mediterranean and other ethnic diets in which peppers and chillies are indispensable.

Many of the ensuing recipes are traditionally served in various parts of the world where hot and sweet peppers are highly esteemed.

PART
TWO
· · · · · · · · · ·

Sweetcorn and Red Pepper Salad
· · · · · · · · · ·

Serve this colourful, crunchy salad in late summer and early autumn, when peppers, tomatoes and corn are all at their sweetest and most succulent. Serves four.

2 cobs of sweetcorn
2 sweet red peppers
2 sticks (ribs) of celery, thinly sliced
1 clove of garlic, peeled and finely chopped
3-4 juicy tomatoes, washed and sliced
8 leaves of rocket (rucola, arugula), washed
handful of flat-leaved parsley, washed
3 tbs extra virgin olive oil
1 tbs red wine vinegar
pinch of salt
shavings of parmesan

Remove all the husks and fibres from the cobs and slice each row of kernels vertically with a sharp knife. Slice the kernels off the cobs. Put them in a pan with a little water and bring to the boil. Cook for about 8 minutes, or until tender. Drain well and reserve. Meanwhile, remove the caps, pith and seeds of the peppers. Finely dice the flesh. Combine all the ingredients except the oil, vinegar, salt and parmesan in a serving bowl, and mix thoroughly. Beat the oil with the vinegar and salt and pour over the salad. Mix well. Cover with shavings of parmesan, and serve.

MIXED PEPPERS SALAD

· · · · · · · · · ·

Try to use peppers of different colours for maximum visual impact; ideally, include at least three of the following colours: purple, red, green, yellow, orange and white. Serves four with a selection of other antipasti.

4 sweet peppers
2 cloves of garlic, peeled and finely chopped
handful of fresh parsley, washed and chopped
4 tbs extra virgin olive oil
juice of half a lemon
salt
freshly milled black pepper

Grill (broil) or roast the peppers until the skins are uniformly black and blistered. Transfer them to a bowl, cover and leave to cool. Slip off the skins, trim away the white pith and seeds and slice the flesh into long strips about 1cm/^{2}/$_5$ inch wide. Transfer them to a serving bowl.

Sprinkle with the garlic and parsley. Beat the olive oil with the lemon juice and pour over the salad. Season and mix well. Serve within 24 hours, with crusty bread.

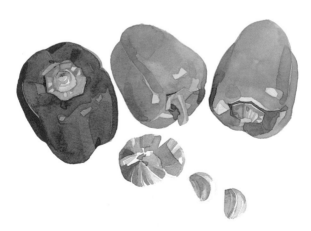

AROMATIC PEPPER SAUCE
• • • • • • • • • •

Multi-coloured peppers combined with tomatoes, aubergines (eggplants), and black olives and scented with fresh basil result in an attractive and aromatic sauce for pasta.

1 red pepper
1 yellow or orange pepper
1 green pepper
6 tbs fruity olive oil
1 small aubergine, cut into small cubes
medium onion, peeled and chopped
2 cloves of garlic, peeled and finely chopped
400g/14oz durum wheat pasta
4 ripe, fresh or canned peeled plum tomatoes, chopped
salt
freshly milled black pepper
12 black olives, pitted
handful of fresh basil leaves

Wash the peppers and pat them dry. Remove their caps, seeds and white membranes; dice their flesh.

Heat the olive oil in a non-stick frying pan and fry the aubergine cubes over a high heat, lightly browning them evenly. Transfer them to a plate lined with paper towels. Gently sauté the onion until soft and lightly coloured. Add the garlic and peppers and mix well. Cover the pan. Cook the peppers gently until soft, stirring occasionally (10–15 minutes).

Meanwhile, immerse 400g/14oz of durum wheat pasta of your choice in plenty of salted boiling water; mix, and boil until *al dente*.

Meanwhile, add the tomatoes and aubergines to the pan with the peppers. Season, and cook uncovered until the tomatoes have released their liquid and the sauce has thickened. Add the olives and cook for a minute longer. Drain the pasta, transfer it to a warm serving dish and mix thoroughly with the sauce. Tear up and add the basil; mix again. Serve.

Sweet Pepper Purée

· · · · · · · · · ·

This slightly sweet sauce (with an optional gentle bite of chilli) is very good with pasta or as a sauce for fish and poultry. Sufficient for four portions, it can be made in advance and refrigerated in a covered container, until required.

4 red peppers
4 tbs olive oil
1 small onion, peeled and chopped
1 clove of garlic, peeled and chopped
1 fresh or dried chilli, seeded and chopped (optional)
4 tbs chopped tomatoes
salt
freshly milled black pepper
1 tsp sugar
handful of fresh parsley, washed and chopped

Remove the peppers' piths, seeds and caps.

Stew all the vegetables gently in the oil for about 12 minutes. Season, add the sugar and parsley, mix well, and allow the mixture to cool. Process in a food processor and re-heat briefly when required.

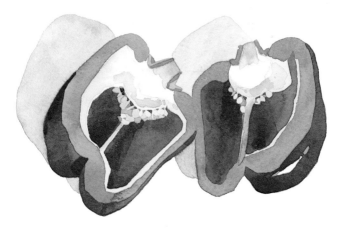

SWEET PEPPER CROSTINI
· · · · · · · · · ·

Red, yellow and orange sweet pepper fillets look attractive together, but any single colour works just as well if others are unavailable. These crostini are delicious in a whole spread of antipasti, or served just with a salad as a light appetizer. This recipe makes eight crostini, enough for four people.

loaf of crusty bread
1 red pepper
1 yellow pepper
1 orange pepper
1 clove of garlic, peeled and finely chopped
3 ripe tomatoes, diced
handful of fresh parsley, washed and chopped
salt
110ml/4fl oz/$\frac{1}{2}$ cup extra virgin olive oil
1 clove of garlic, peeled and left whole
freshly milled black pepper

Cut 8 slices of bread, each about 2cm/1 inch thick.

Grill (broil) the peppers until the skins are uniformly black and blistered. Transfer to a bowl, cover, and let them steam until they are cool enough to touch. Remove and discard the skins, seeds and pithy membrane. Dice the flesh and transfer to a clean bowl. Combine with the chopped garlic and tomato, parsley and salt. Drizzle with 2 tbs of the olive oil, reserving about 6 tbs to dress the crostini. (This can be done several hours ahead; in fact, the flavours will deepen.)

Pre-heat an oven to 220°C/425°F/gas mark 7. Bake the bread lightly until golden (this will take just a few minutes). Crush the whole garlic clove and rub one side of the bread slices with it. Spoon a layer of the pepper mixture over each rubbed slice, and drizzle with the remaining olive oil. Grind a little black pepper over each. Bake again briefly without burning the bread, and serve hot.

ROASTED PEPPERS WITH ANCHOVIES

A very simple and delicious Spanish tapa to serve with chilled fino sherry or ice-cold beer, combining the distinctive flavours of sweet, tender roasted peppers, anchovies and fruity olive oil. Use only very red and fleshy fresh bell peppers or pimientoes, or preserved pepper fillets. This makes 16–18 individual rounds.

1 large baguette loaf
2 red peppers
small can of plump anchovy fillets in oil
freshly milled black pepper
extra virgin olive oil

Slice the bread into thin rounds. Lightly toast them under the grill (broiler). Roast the peppers over a high flame or under the grill until the skins blister and blacken. Leave them to steam in a covered bowl until cool enough to touch.

Slip off the skins and scrape away the seeds. Slice off the white membranes and slice the fillets into strips the width of your little finger. Place two or three strips of pepper over each round of toasted bread and cover each one with an anchovy fillet. Grind a little black pepper over each tapa and finish with a few drops of olive oil.

MEATLESS STUFFED PEPPERS

If orange or yellow peppers are unavailable, just use red ones. Serves six vegetarians as an appetizer or light lunch.

6 sweet peppers (red, orange or yellow or a combination)
olive oil, for frying
1 medium onion, peeled and finely chopped
2 cloves of garlic, peeled and chopped
400g/14oz can of plum tomatoes. chopped
salt
freshly milled black pepper
8 tbs pine nuts, lightly toasted in a dry pan
8 tbs breadcrumbs
250g/9oz/1 1/2 cups cooked rice
generous handful of parsley, washed and chopped
4 tbs white wine
6 tbs grated cheese
110ml/4fl oz/1/2 cup water, or white wine
4 tbs olive oil

Remove the caps and seeds of the peppers.

Heat a shallow layer of olive oil in a non-stick or well-seasoned frying pan and fry the peppers in batches until the skins have coloured slightly. Remove and allow them to cool a little. Wipe them with paper towels. Re-heat the oil and sauté the onion until it has softened and coloured a little. Add the garlic and the tomatoes, season, and simmer for about 6 minutes. Preheat the oven to 200°C/400°F/gas mark 6.

Make the stuffing by combining the pine nuts, half of the breadcrumbs and half of the cooked tomato mixture, a little more salt and black pepper, rice, parsley and white wine. Mix everything thoroughly. Stuff the peppers with the mixture and stand them upright side by side in two oven dishes. Top with the remaining tomato pulp and breadcrumbs and all the grated cheese. Pour over a little water or white wine, drizzle with olive oil and bake for about 45 minutes, or until the peppers are soft.

TRADITIONAL STUFFED PEPPERS
· · · · · · · · · ·

In this recipe the peppers are stuffed with a more traditional mixture of minced beef or lamb and cooked
rice that is used to stuff all manner of vegetables
throughout the Mediterranean, the Balkans and the
Middle East. Serves six as an appetizer.

6 sweet peppers (red, orange or yellow or a combination)
6 tbs extra virgin olive oil
1 small onion, peeled and diced
2 cloves of garlic, peeled and finely chopped
110g/4oz lean minced beef or lamb
salt
freshly milled black pepper
pinch of ground cumin
175g/6oz/1 cup cooked rice
generous handful of fresh parsley
1 fresh or canned plum tomato, peeled and chopped
3 tbs pine nuts, lightly toasted
200g/7oz fresh or canned peeled plum tomatoes, chopped
6 tbs water

Remove the caps and seeds of the peppers.
    Heat 2 tbs of oil in a large frying pan and briefly
fry the peppers. Allow them to cool and wipe them with
paper towels; stand them upright in oven dishes. Pre-
heat the oven to 200°C/400°F/gas mark 6.
    Re-heat the oil and fry the onion. Add the garlic
and the minced meat; increase the heat and stir-fry for
about 6 minutes. Season well with the salt, pepper and
cumin. Turn off the heat. Add the cooked rice, parsley,
chopped tomato and pine nuts, and mix very thoroughly. Spoon the mixture into the fried peppers,
packing it down. Sprinkle the remaining 4 tbs of olive
oil over the stuffed peppers, spread the remaining
chopped tomatoes over them, and pour in enough water
(about 6 tbs) to come a little way up the sides. Bake for
about 45 minutes, or until the peppers are tender and
lightly browned.

MUSHROOM GULYAS
. . . .

In Hungary, many different ingredients are cooked with paprika, including wild mushrooms which Hungarians hold in high esteem. The rich sauce will elevate even ordinary cultivated button mushrooms to a higher plane of enjoyment. Serves four as an appetizer, or two as a light lunch or supper, accompanied by rice, noodles, or lightly baked slices of brioche bread.

4 tbs olive oil
110g/4oz shallots, peeled and chopped
2 cloves of garlic, peeled and finely chopped
$\frac{1}{2}$ tsp caraway seeds
400g/14oz mushrooms, thickly sliced
salt
1 tbs paprika
$\frac{1}{2}$ tsp cayenne
1 tbs bottled tomato passata, *or*
1 canned plum tomato, chopped
3 tbs white wine
6 heaped tbs unsweetened fromage frais
a few drops of lemon juice
1-2 sprigs of fresh dill, washed and chopped

Heat the olive oil and sweat the shallots until they are soft. Add the garlic and caraway seeds, stir, and add the mushrooms. Raise the heat and fry them for 4–5 minutes, stirring constantly. Season with salt, paprika and cayenne, add the tomato and wine, mix well, and simmer for 3 minutes, or until the sauce has thickened. Add the fromage frais and lemon juice and heat through. Sprinkle with dill and serve.

PIZZA ALLA SICILIANA

· · · · · · · · · ·

This thin pizza dough crisps on baking and is an authentic version of the thin pizzas Italians eat. The topping is a delicious combination of mozzarella, tomato, spicy peperone sausage, chillies, and fresh basil. Small domestic ovens require large, rigid baking sheets or oven pans to accommodate the pizzas. The dough can be kneaded by hand or with a machine fitted with dough hooks. This makes four smallish pizzas. The same recipe can be used to make more mini pizzas. Just divide the dough into smaller balls and roll each one out into discs 7cm/2$\frac{1}{2}$ inches in diameter, and reduce the baking time to prevent them from burning.

Dough
$\frac{1}{2}$ packet of yeast (about 1$\frac{1}{2}$ tsp)
225ml/8fl oz/1 cup hot water
350g/12oz/3 cups plain (all-purpose) flour
1 tsp salt
1 tbs olive oil

Dissolve the yeast in the water. Mix the flour, salt and olive oil in a bowl. Gradually add the yeast mixture, kneading all the while by hand, or by machine. When the dough is smooth and elastic, transfer it to an oiled container, cover with a clean cloth and leave to rest somewhere warm for an hour, or until it has doubled in size. Dust your hands, a work surface and a rolling pin with flour. Divide the dough into two balls and divide each ball into two. Roll out the four dough balls into discs about 20–23cm/8–9 inches in diameter, turning the dough to ensure circular shapes.

Pre-heat the oven to 220°C/425°F/gas mark 7.

Topping
225ml/8fl oz/1 cup bottled tomato passata
2 packets of Italian mozzarella (300g/11oz in total), diced
60g/3oz sliced Italian peperone sausage
4 mild fresh or pickled green chillies, seeded and roughly
chopped
8 large basil leaves
salt
freshly milled black pepper
olive oil

Place the pizzas on two well-oiled flat baking sheets. Alternatively, place them in a large, oiled oven pan, or in individual oiled tart pans. Spread a quarter of the tomato pulp on each, spreading it out so as to all but cover the pizza surface. Dot evenly with mozzarella. Divide the peperone slices between the four pizzas. Sprinkle with the chillies and some freshly torn basil leaves. Season well and drizzle a little olive oil over each pizza. Bake in the oven on two shelves for 15–20 minutes. Check the dough to ensure that the edges and base are firm and lightly browned – you may have to swap the trays to ensure that all four pizzas are evenly cooked.

Pizza alla Giardiniera

This pizza takes its name from the garden vegetables that go into the topping, a delicious combination of peppers, tomatoes and peas, combined with ham, eggs and mozzarella cheese. Serves four.

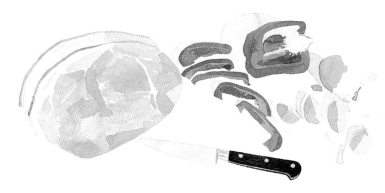

110ml/4fl oz/$^{1}/_{2}$ cup bottled tomato passata
skinned fillets of 2 whole red peppers, sliced into strips
110g/4oz shelled fresh or (thawed) frozen peas
200g/7oz Italian mozzarella, diced
4 fresh tomatoes, sliced
110g/4oz thinly sliced cooked ham
4 hard-boiled (hard-cooked) eggs, shelled and quartered
olive oil
salt
freshly milled black pepper

Make the pizza dough following the basic recipe. Roll it out into four pizzas. Pre-heat the oven to 220°C/425°F/gas mark 7.

Spread a thin layer of tomato pulp over each pizza. Cover with the pepper strips and peas, distributed evenly. Dot with mozzarella. Place the tomato slices and the pieces of ham and cooked egg over each pizza. Drizzle with olive oil, and season. Bake for 15–20 minutes, following the basic advice given in the previous recipe.

Patatas al Pimentón

A mouth-tingling dish of potatoes cooked with paprika and spices to accompany drinks, or to serve with a selection of tapas.

1kg/2¼ lb potatoes
pinch of saffron
6 tbs chicken stock (broth)
olive oil, for frying
2 cloves
small piece of cinnamon
2 bay leaves
2 sprigs of fresh rosemary
2 tbs mild paprika
1 tsp cayenne
salt
4 canned plum tomatoes, crushed
handful of fresh parsley, washed and chopped.

If necessary wash the potatoes to remove all traces of dirt. Do not peel them, but cut them into cubes each about 2cm/1 inch square. Infuse the saffron in the hot stock for about 10 minutes.

Heat a layer of olive oil in a non-stick frying pan and fry the potatoes with the cloves, cinnamon, bay and rosemary until the potatoes are golden (test with a fork to check that the centres are soft). Pour off as much of the oil as possible, reserving it for future use. Add the paprika and cayenne, season, and pour in the stock and tomatoes. Mix well, cover, and cook over a low heat for about 5 minutes. Sprinkle with parsley and serve hot or warm.

Spaghetti with Sweet Peppers

S weet peppers, onions, capers, anchovies and olive
oil – these ingredients are redolent of southern Italy
and Sicily where vegetables and fish are especially
relished with durum wheat pasta. Serves four.

4 sweet red peppers
400g/14oz spaghetti
110ml/4fl oz/¹/₂ cup olive oil
1 medium onion, peeled and chopped
3 cloves of garlic, peeled and finely chopped
2 tsp capers, rinsed and drained
4 anchovy fillets in oil
salt
freshly milled black pepper
generous handful of fresh parsley, washed and chopped
freshly grated pecorino cheese

Grill (broil) the peppers, or roast over a naked flame until the skins have blistered and blackened. Cover and allow them to steam until they have cooled sufficiently to touch. Slip off and discard the skins. Slice off the white membrane and scrape away the seeds. Cut the flesh into finger-sized strips.

Bring a very large pot of salted water to a rolling boil. Immerse the spaghetti and mix well. Boil for about 12 minutes, or until *al dente*.

Meanwhile, heat half of the oil in a pan. Sauté the onion until it colours a little (about 5 minutes). Add the garlic, capers, and anchovies. Mix well, season, and add the peppers. Sauté them for about 5 minutes, while the pasta continues to cook. Sprinkle with the parsley and mix well.

Drain the pasta and transfer to a warm serving dish. Toss with the remaining olive oil and the peppers. Serve immediately with a bowl of freshly grated pecorino cheese, and crusty bread.

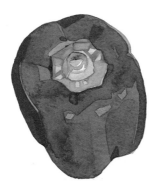

FUSILLI ALL' ARRABBIATA
· · · · · · · · · · ·

O ther curved or ribbed pasta shapes such as spiral-li, penne rigati or rigatoni can be substituted for fusilli. *Arrabbiata* means 'enraged', an effect of the fiery chillies reflected in the angry red colour of the tomato sauce. When in season in late summer, try to use really ripe fresh plum tomatoes; at all other times it is better to substitute good quality canned plum tomatoes. Any left over pasta is delicious cold, tossed in additional olive oil and fresh chopped parsley. Serves four, with crusty bread.

350g/12oz factory-made pasta
4 tbs fruity olive oil
1 small red onion, peeled and chopped
2 fresh medium-hot chillies, finely sliced, *or*
2 small dried red chillies, crumbled
450g/1lb fresh plum tomatoes, peeled and diced, *or*
400g/14oz can of plum tomatoes, chopped
3 cloves of garlic, peeled and finely chopped
salt
handful of fresh parsley, washed and chopped
freshly grated parmesan cheese (optional)

Bring plenty of salted water to a rolling boil in a very large pot. Immerse the pasta.

Meanwhile, prepare the sauce. Heat the olive oil in a pan. Sauté the onion until soft, then add the chillies, tomatoes and garlic. Season, mix well and simmer while the pasta cooks. When the pasta is *al dente* and the sauce has thickened, drain the pasta and combine with the sauce. Sprinkle with parsley, mix well and serve with crusty bread and, if desired, with parmesan cheese.

Rainbow Fried Rice

. . . .

This attractive multi-coloured dish calls for cold, cooked rice. Serves six as a complete course on its own.

5 tbs peanut oil
4 eggs, beaten
pinch of salt
225g/8oz lean ham or bacon, diced
2 carrots, scrubbed and finely diced
350g/12oz chestnut or oyster mushrooms, sliced
1 large red pepper, seeded and trimmed, diced
2 hot green chillies, washed and thinly sliced
2 cloves of garlic, peeled and chopped
6 spring onions (scallions), sliced
200g/7oz bean sprouts
1110g/2½lb cooked long grain rice
4 tbs light soy sauce
2 lettuce hearts, shredded
2 tbs sesame oil

Heat 1 tbs of the oil in a non-stick frying pan. Make a small omelette with the eggs, adding a pinch of salt. Lift the omelette from the pan and cut it into strips. Reserve.

Heat the remaining oil in a wok to smoking point. Stir-fry the ham or bacon for 30 seconds. Add the carrots, mix well, and add the mushrooms, pepper and chillies, and the garlic and white sections of the spring onions (reserve the green sections), mixing well after each addition. Stir-fry these ingredients for a minute or so. Add the bean sprouts and stir-fry for 30 seconds longer. Now tip in all the rice, breaking up any lumps with the wok scoop, and combine thoroughly with the stir-fried ingredients. Heat through. Add the soy sauce and stir-fry for 30 seconds. Add the shredded lettuce hearts and mix thoroughly. Transfer to a warm serving dish and decorate with the strips of omelette. Sprinkle with sesame oil and scatter over the green spring onions. Serve immediately.

Sweet Pepper Risotto

. . . .

Serve this colourful and delicious risotto as an appetizer for four. Alternatively, the quantities will
serve two hungry people as a complete lunch or supper dish. It is worth keeping a supply of home-made
skinned and seeded sweet red peppers which can be
preserved in oil in a jar and kept in the fridge (see
below).

2 large red peppers, skinned and seeded
1 litre/2^1/$_4$ pints/4^1/$_2$ cups chicken or vegetable
stock (broth)
5 tbs olive oil
1 medium onion, peeled and chopped
1 small stick (rib) of celery, washed and diced
2 cloves of garlic, peeled and chopped
275g/10oz peeled fresh or canned plum tomatoes, chopped
salt
freshly milled black pepper
275g/10 oz/1^1/$_2$ cups arborio rice
110g/4oz freshly grated parmesan cheese
handful of fresh parsley, washed and chopped

Dice the peppers, discarding the pithy membranes.
Bring the stock to a gentle simmer in a covered pan.

Heat the olive oil in a large, shallow pan. Fry the
onion and celery until they have turned pale gold. Add
the garlic and mix well. Pour in the tomatoes and add
the diced peppers. Season, mix well, and fry for a
minute longer. Add the rice and stir to coat with the
sauce for a minute or two. Add the hot stock in stages,
stirring well with each addition. (The rice will absorb
the liquid readily and should be allowed almost to dry
out before more is added.) Continue until all the stock
has been used, the rice is soft, but retains a very slight
firmness, and is no longer soupy (this will take about
25 minutes). Transfer to a warm serving platter, mix
in half of the grated parmesan and all the parsley. Serve
with the remaining parmesan.

Home-made bell pepper fillets

Grill (broil) three or four large, very red peppers until
the skin is uniformly black and blistered. Let them cool
in a covered bowl (the steam loosens the skins). When
they are cool enough to touch, remove the skins which
will slip off very easily. Scrape off the seeds and trim
off the white inner membranes. Put the fillets into a
large clean jar previously sterilized by immersion in
freshly boiled water. Top up with enough olive oil com-
pletely to cover the fillets and screw on the lid. Keep
in the fridge and consume within a week.

Risotto croquettes

Use up any surplus risotto to make delectable fried cro-
quettes: just mix in a little flour, shape with floured
hands into the shapes of small sausages or golf balls,
roll them in additional flour, and deep or shallow fry
in olive oil until evenly golden.

HOT AND SOUR SOUP

A uthenticity calls for chicken's or duck's blood and diced pork, but this vegetarian version of a very popular peasant soup from northern China includes plenty of bean curd, dried and fresh mushrooms, and a dash of bitingly hot chilli oil (available bottled in Oriental stores, or see the recipe in this book). The soup is garnished with aromatic coriander (cilantro) and sliced green chillies, for extra bite. As one might imagine, this is exceptionally warming in cold weather and is guaranteed to clear blocked noses, while the shiitake and oyster mushrooms are believed to reduce high blood pressure. Serves four or six.

40g/1½oz dried shiitake mushrooms
25g/1oz thin rice noodles
1 litre/2¼ pints/4½ cups chicken stock (broth)
60g/3oz fresh young oyster mushrooms, diced
250g/9oz fresh bean curd cakes, diced
2 tbs light soy sauce
1 tbs dark soy sauce
4 tbs rice vinegar
2 tbs Shaohsing wine, or sherry
2 tsp sugar
salt
freshly milled black pepper
4 spring onions (scallions), thinly sliced
1 tbs flour mixed with 2 tbs water
2 eggs, beaten
1 tbs sesame oil
1-2 tsp chilli oil (to taste)
handful of fresh coriander (cilantro), washed and chopped
2-3 green chillies, seeded and thinly sliced (optional)

Soak the dried mushrooms in warm water for 30 minutes to reconstitute them. Strain and reserve the water. Slice the shiitake caps very thinly, discarding the tough stalks. Meanwhile, bring a pot of water to the boil. Immerse the noodles and boil for the recommended period (usually 3–5 minutes). Drain and reserve them.

Bring the stock and the mushrooms' soaking liquid to a boil in a large pot. Add the reconstituted and fresh mushrooms, the noodles, bean curd, soy sauces, vinegar, Shaohsing wine, sugar, seasoning, and the spring onions. Return to the boil, reduce the heat, and simmer for 3–4 minutes, then add the flour dissolved in water, stir, and allow the soup to thicken a little. Stir in the beaten eggs in a very thin stream, stretching them as they set. Add the sesame and chilli oils, mix, and simmer for a minute longer. Serve garnished with the coriander and green chillies.

Szechuan Fish-fragrant Aubergines (Eggplants)
··········

Peppercorns and chillies; rice vinegar; sugar; soy sauce – the classic hot, sour, sweet and salty flavourings of Szechuan are used to cook fish, hence the name of this delicious aubergine dish. Serves four with plain rice and one or two other Oriental dishes.

2 tsp Szechuan peppercorns (or crushed black peppercorns)
4-6 hot, dried red chillies
1 tbs canned yellow beans, mashed
700g/1½lb small aubergines
225ml/8fl oz/1 cup peanut oil
4 cloves of garlic, peeled and chopped
2cm/1 inch piece of fresh ginger, peeled and finely chopped
4 spring onions (scallions), washed and sliced into thick sections
2 tbs rice vinegar
2 tbs Shaohsing wine, or dry sherry
1 tbs sugar
2 tbs soy sauce
6 tbs water
2 tbs sesame oil

Lightly toast the Szechuan peppercorns in a heavy pan. Grind them with a mortar and pestle or in a clean coffee grinder and pass them through a wire strainer, discarding the husks. (Grind the black peppercorns coarsely, if using.) Grind the chillies, seeds and all. Transfer the ground ingredients to a bowl and mix well with the mashed yellow beans.

Slice the aubergines obliquely once, if they are very small, or into chunks each about 4cm/2 inches x 2cm/1 inch. Heat the oil in a wok to smoking point. Add the aubergines and stir-fry them in two batches, until golden (2–3 minutes). Remove them with a slotted spoon and transfer to a plate lined with paper towels. Pour off most of the oil, leaving a layer to cover the base of the wok. Add the garlic and ginger, stir, and add the spring onions (white sections only – reserve the green leaves), and the chilli and peppercorn paste. Stir, and return the aubergines to the wok. Toss them in the paste, to coat. Add the rice vinegar and Shaohsing wine, the sugar, soy sauce, and water. Cook over a high heat until the sauce thickens a little, (2–3 more minutes) and serve, sprinkled with sesame oil and the green spring onion sections.

CHILLI BEEF NOODLES

T hese spicy Chinese noodles enriched with morsels of meltingly tender marinated beef can be made with large, mild varieties of chillies, or with a combination of hot chillies and green peppers. This serves two hungry people, as a light lunch or supper, or four as an appetizer, or accompanied by other Oriental dishes.

4 large mild green chillies *or*
1 small green pepper *and* 2-3 hot fresh chillies
110g/4oz fillet or rump of beef
6 tbs peanut oil
½ tsp sugar
2 tsp Shaohsing wine, or dry sherry
1 tbs soy sauce
250g/9oz dried egg noodles
110g/4oz broccoli, cut into small florets
4 cloves of garlic, peeled and finely chopped
2cm/1 inch piece of fresh ginger, peeled and finely chopped
110g/4oz mushrooms, thinly sliced
1 tbs rice vinegar
4 spring onions (scallions), washed and sliced
1 ripe tomato, peeled and chopped
1 tbs sesame oil
50g/2oz cashews, lightly crushed

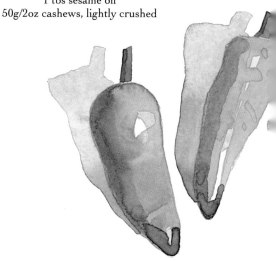

Wash the chillies and green pepper (if using). Remove their seeds and slice them thinly. Trim the beef and slice it into thin strips. Put the beef in a bowl and combine with 2 tbs peanut oil and the sugar, wine and soy sauce, stirring well.

Bring plenty of water to the boil in a pot. Immerse the egg noodles and let the water return to the boil. Turn off the heat. Let the noodles rest in the water for about 5 minutes. Remove and drain them. (If the noodles are still hard, continue to boil them until *al dente*.) Toss the noodles in a little oil. Bring the water back to the boil and immerse the broccoli for a minute. Refresh under cold running water and drain well.

Heat the remaining oil in a wok. Add the garlic and ginger, toss in the oil for 30 seconds, then add the chillies. Stir-fry for 30 seconds. Add the mushrooms and broccoli and stir-fry for a minute. Add the beef and its marinade, the rice vinegar, spring onions and tomato. Mix well and cook for another minute, stirring all the while. Add the noodles, mix well and stir-fry for one more minute. Transfer to a hot serving platter and sprinkle with the sesame oil and crushed cashews. Serve immediately.

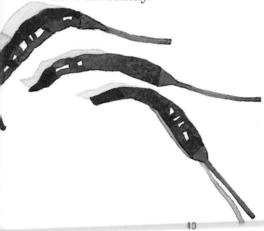

STIR-FRIED BEEF WITH GREEN PEPPERS

. . . .

Tender beef and crunchy green peppers are a wonderful combination. The beef is flavoured by a brief period of marination, quickly stir-fried, and finished in a chilli sauce. Delicious with plenty of plain boiled rice, this serves four.

Marinade
450g/1lb lean rump of beef, trimmed
2 tbs light soy sauce
2 tbs dark soy sauce
1 tsp sugar
1 tbs Shaohsing wine
1 tbs sesame oil

Sauce
4 tbs water
3 tbs bottled Chinese chilli sauce
1 tbs Shaohsing wine
2 tbs light soy sauce

4 tbs peanut oil
4 cloves of garlic, peeled and thinly sliced
2cm/1 inch piece of fresh ginger, peeled and finely chopped
2 small green peppers, seeded and roughly chopped
2 fresh hot chillies, seeded and thinly sliced
white part of 1 leek, sliced in thick sections
1 tbs sesame oil

Cut the beef into thin strips. Place them in a bowl with the rest of the marinade ingredients and mix thoroughly. Set aside for at least 30 minutes.

Combine all the sauce ingredients and mix them well. Remove the beef from the marinade.

Heat the oil in a wok. When smoking, add the garlic and ginger, mix once, and add the peppers and chillies. Stir-fry for a minute and add the beef. Mix well and add the leek. Stir-fry for 30 seconds. Stir the sauce and pour it into the wok, stirring until the sauce has thickened (2–3 minutes). Mix in the sesame oil and serve straight away.

GUACAMOLE

· · · · · · · · · ·

A vocados have been cultivated in Mexico for millennia, and were gathered in the wild eight thousand years ago. The Aztecs combined them with tomatoes and capsicums and so invented guacamole. Good guacamole should conceal a distinctly hot bite beneath its initial cool silkiness. Serves four as a dip for crudités and soft tortillas, or as a topping for re-fried beans and corn tostadas.

3 very ripe tomatoes, peeled and sliced
half a mild onion, peeled and quartered
3 fresh hot green chillies, washed and seeded
1 small green pepper, washed and seeded
juice of 1 lime
2 ripe avocados
salt
1 fresh red chilli, finely sliced (optional)

Grind the tomatoes, onion, chillies and green pepper in a food processor to a smooth soupy paste. Transfer to a bowl with the lime juice. Peel the avocados, remove the stones (pits) and mash the flesh very thoroughly with a fork. Work into the chilli paste, season and mix well. Garnish with the sliced red chilli, if using. Use immediately or cover and eat within an hour.

FRIED CHICKEN WITH CHILLIES
· · · · · · · · · ·

A dapted from a traditional Laotian recipe, this thick
chicken curry is typical of many such dishes from
south east Asia in the use of fried shallots and chillies
as garnishes. Serves four with plenty of plain boiled
rice and a stir-fried vegetable.

large corn-fed or free-range chicken
1 small red onion, peeled
6 tbs peanut oil
8 green chillies, seeded and halved vertically
6 small red shallots, peeled and chopped
6 spring onions (scallions), washed and thickly sliced
4 cloves of garlic, peeled and chopped
280 ml/10fl oz/1 1/4 cups canned coconut milk
2 tbs fish sauce
2 tbs light soy sauce
handful of fresh coriander (cilantro), chopped

Skin the chicken; cut each of the boned breasts into 2
or 3 sections. Cut the flesh off the legs. Discard the
carcass, or reserve it to make stock (broth). Halve
the onion from top to bottom. Slice each half into thin
half-rings.

Heat 2 tbs of the oil in a wok and fry the chillies
briefly. Reserve them.

Add the remaining oil to the wok; fry the shallots
until browned. Remove them with a slotted spoon and
reserve them.

Re-heat the oil until it smokes. Fry the chicken
pieces until golden. Add the onion and continue to stir-
fry for a minute longer. Add the white parts of the
spring onions and the garlic, mix, and pour in the
coconut milk and the fish and soy sauces. Mix well.
Simmer until the chicken is cooked and the sauce has
thickened (about 15 minutes). Transfer to a serving
bowl, mix in the fried shallots, chillies and coriander
and serve.

CHICKEN PAPRIKAS
· · · · · · · · · ·

Hungarian paprika sometimes has a hot bite. Similar results can be obtained with common sweet paprika and a pinch of cayenne. Other ingredients – veal, beef, fish fillets – can be prepared equally successfully this way, if cooking times are adjusted accordingly. Ordinary single (light) cream can be soured with the addition of a few drops of lemon juice, or substitute crème fraîche. Serves four.

1 green pepper, washed
1 large, corn-fed or free-range chicken
4 tbs sunflower oil
1 large onion, peeled and chopped
3 cloves of garlic, peeled and chopped
salt
1 tbs paprika
$1/2$ tsp cayenne, or less, according to taste
2 large, very ripe tomatoes, peeled and chopped
4 tbs water
4 tbs soured cream

Remove the cap and seeds of the pepper, cut away the pithy membrane and discard these. Dice the flesh. Cut the chicken into serving pieces.

Heat the oil in a large, heavy pot. Brown the chicken pieces evenly, and reserve them. Add the onion and fry until golden. Add the garlic and stir. Return the chicken pieces, season, and add the pepper, paprika and cayenne (if using). Stir, and add the tomatoes. Cook them over a high heat for 2 more minutes, stirring constantly, then add the water. Reduce the heat, cover and simmer for 25 minutes, stirring occasionally. Add the soured cream, heat through, and serve with fresh noodles, potatoes, or rice.

POULET BASQUAISE

$\cdot \cdot \cdot \cdot \cdot \cdot \cdot \cdot \cdot \cdot$

This colourful dish is from the Basses Pyrénées-France's Basque country. A local adoration of peppers is evident in the many specialities of the region, such as pipérade, the fishermen's soup known as *ttoro*, the renowned hams of Bayonne that are rubbed with red peppers and coated in rock salt, and *chipirons* (tender baby squid in paprika). So popular are fresh and dried peppers here that throughout France dishes with the suffix *à la basquaise* are guaranteed to have been cooked with peppers. Serves four.

4 tbs olive oil
1 large corn-fed or free-range chicken, jointed
1 small onion, peeled and diced
60g/3oz Bayonne, Parma or serrano ham, diced
2 cloves of garlic, peeled and finely chopped
1 green pepper, seeded and diced
1 red pepper, seeded and diced
2 very ripe tomatoes, peeled and finely chopped
4 tbs white wine
salt
freshly milled black pepper

Heat the olive oil in a heavy casserole. Fry the chicken pieces until evenly golden. Remove and reserve them.

Fry the onion until lightly coloured, add the ham, and fry for a minute or two longer. Add the garlic and mix well. Return the chicken to the casserole, add the peppers, tomatoes and wine, season well, and continue to cook for 20–25 more minutes. Serve with mashed or sautéed potatoes.

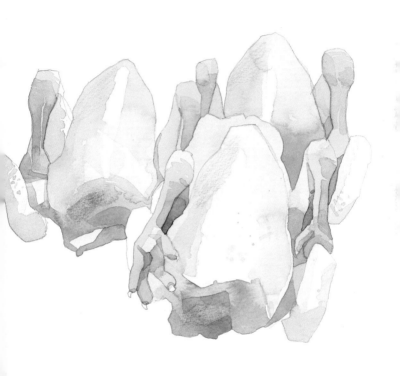

La Pipérade

Béarnaise *pipérade* (the dish is called *piparrada* in the Spanish Basque country) makes a delightful light summer's lunch or supper, or an elegant appetizer. Traditionally made with green peppers, a combination of red and green peppers adds colour. (There is a remarkably similar vegetarian dish called *menemen*, which is also the name of a town in western Turkey.) Serves four with crusty bread or croûtons, and a salad.

50g/2oz sliced Bayonne, Parma or serrano ham
4 tbs fruity olive oil
1 medium onion, peeled and finely chopped
2 cloves of garlic, peeled and finely chopped
1 large red and green pepper, *or*
2 large green peppers, seeded and diced
8 very ripe fresh plum tomatoes, peeled and chopped
salt
freshly milled black pepper
7-8 free-range eggs (depending on size)
pinch of salt
25g/1oz butter

Trim and dice the ham. Heat the oil in a large, well-seasoned frying pan and add the onion. Sauté gently until it has softened and coloured a little. Add the garlic and peppers and cook gently for 10–15 minutes, stirring often. Add the tomatoes and cook until they have given off all their liquid and the sauce has thickened (about 10 more minutes). Season. (Can be prepared in advance up to this point.)

Beat the eggs in a bowl with a little salt. Melt the butter in the pan with the pepper mixture. Pour in the eggs and start scrambling them with a fork. Add the ham and mix thoroughly. Continue to scramble until the eggs have almost set but remain moist. Divide into four portions and serve immediately.

MEXICAN RICE WITH CHILLIES

· · · · · · · · · ·

Until the Spanish conquistadors introduced rice into Mexico, tortillas made from corn flour, and bean pastes similar to today's national dish of re-fried beans provided the ubiquitous and relatively bland starchy foil to hot chilli sauces. Now Mexicans and other Central Americans regularly also eat rice. This dish is similar to many rustic rice dishes of Spain, although the preferred chillies are replaced there by sweet peppers; both were Aztec foods. Serve with hot Mexican stews and sauces, or try this rice *a la cubana*, accompanied by a hot tomato salsa, fried bananas, and a covering of fried eggs (one per person). This quantity serves four.

1 medium onion
4 fresh mild, green chillies
4 tbs sunflower oil
2 cloves of garlic, peeled and finely chopped
1 ripe tomato, peeled and diced
50g/2oz chorizo sausage, finely chopped
bay leaf
350g/12oz/2 cups short-grained rice
900ml/2 pints/4 cups stock (broth)
pinch of salt

Peel the onion. Slice it in half, from top to bottom, and slice each half thinly. Wash the chillies. Split them lengthways and remove the seeds.

Heat the oil in a large, well-seasoned frying pan. Fry the onion until it has softened. Add the garlic, tomato, chorizo sausage and bay leaf, and the split chillies. Fry for 2–3 minutes, then add the rice, mix well and stir-fry for a minute or two longer. Add all the stock, and season. Reduce the heat and simmer, uncovered, until all the liquid has been absorbed and the rice is tender, adding a little water if necessary. Let it stand off the heat for a few minutes before serving.

Tomato salsa

Heat the chopped contents of a 400g/14oz can of tomatoes with 2 tbs olive oil and 1 tbs wine vinegar; add 2 cloves of garlic, peeled and chopped, and 2 dried and crumbled red chillies. Season with salt, and simmer until the tomatoes have thickened.

Fried bananas

Peel 4 bananas. Slice them in half lengthways. Roll them in a little flour and fry them in hot oil in a well-seasoned or non-stick frying pan until uniformly golden-brown. Remove them carefully and transfer to a plate lined with paper towels.

Fry four eggs in very hot olive oil. Transfer the rice to a warm serving platter and top with the fried eggs. Surround with the salsa and fried bananas.

CORDERO AL CHILINDRÓN
· · · · · · · · · ·

*A*l *chilindrón* means 'cooked with peppers', in a manner that is especially identified with the northern
Spanish regions of Navarre and Aragon. The vessel
normally used to stew the lamb and the red peppers
that are a speciality of the region on top of the stove is
an ubiquitous glazed clay pot called a *cazuela*.
Manufactured in a variety of sizes, they are cheap and
extremely versatile. Serves four.

2 large, meaty red peppers
4 tbs fruity olive oil
900g/2lb lamb, trimmed and evenly cubed
freshly milled black pepper
1 large onion, halved vertically and sliced
3 cloves of garlic, peeled and chopped
2 tsp paprika
sprig of thyme
bay leaf
400g/14oz fresh or canned peeled plum tomatoes, chopped
1 tbs red wine vinegar
salt

Grill (broil) the peppers until the skins are uniformly
black and blistered. Transfer them to a bowl and cover.
After 15 minutes or so the peppers will have cooled
enough to touch and the vapour will have loosened the
skins. Remove these without washing the peppers,
scrape off the seeds and trim away the pithy membrane.
Cut the flesh into strips the width of a finger.

Heat the olive oil and fry the lamb on all sides until
browned. Remove to a platter and season with black
pepper. Add the onion and fry until golden. Return the
lamb, add the garlic and stir around for a minute. Add
the paprika, thyme and bay leaf and stir well. Pour in
the tomatoes, add the peppers and vinegar and season
well. Cover, transfer to the smallest hob and simmer
very gently for 2 hours, stirring occasionally. Remove
the herbs and serve with sautéed potatoes.

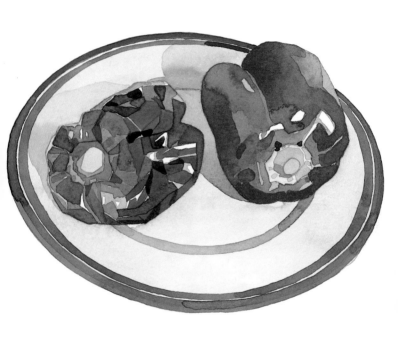

STEWED LAMB WITH GREEN PEPPERS
· · · · · · · · · ·

A daube with a difference – green peppers and aubergines (eggplants) that are added towards the end of the cooking time. Serve with noodles, rice or potatoes; no other vegetable is necessary. Serves four.

6 tbs olive oil
900g/2lb lean lamb, trimmed and evenly cubed
1 large onion, peeled and chopped
1 stick (rib) of celery, washed and finely sliced
1 carrot, scrubbed and finely diced
2 cloves of garlic, peeled and chopped
3 very ripe fresh or canned plum tomatoes, chopped
6 tbs white wine
4 tbs water
salt
freshly milled black pepper
2 bay leaves
2 small, elongated aubergines washed and cubed, *or*
6 baby aubergines, halved
3 green peppers, trimmed, seeded and diced

Heat the olive oil in a heavy pot and brown the lamb in two batches. Remove and reserve it. Fry the onion, celery and carrot until golden, add the garlic, and stir. Return the lamb, mix well, and pour in the tomatoes, wine and water. Season well and add the bay leaves. Reduce the heat, cover, and simmer gently for $1\frac{1}{2}$ hours.

Add the aubergines and peppers, stir, and continue to cook for 30 minutes, stirring occasionally. Serve.

NAM PRIK

· · · · · · · · · ·

Nam prik means 'chilli-hot water', and is a favourite Thai chilli relish that accompanies crisp fried fish. Dried or fresh chillies can be used, preferably tiny Thai 'bird's eye' chillies. Pea aubergines (eggplants) are a little round variety that look like pale peas; fresh ones are sometimes available in specialist Oriental stores, but they are not essential.

8-12 pea aubergines, washed
6 hot chillies, sliced or crumbled
3 cloves of garlic, peeled
$\frac{1}{2}$ stick of lemon grass, washed and sliced
1 tbs sugar
juice of a lime or half a lemon
1 tbs fish sauce

Pluck the aubergines off their stems. Transfer them to a mortar or to the bowl of a food processor. Add the chillies, garlic, lemon grass and sugar; pound or process to a coarse paste, then add the citrus juice and fish sauce, stirring thoroughly to incorporate the liquid. Serve with fried fish and rice or as an exceedingly hot and tangy dip for battered and deep fried vegetables, or crudités and hard boiled (hard cooked) eggs.

PICKLED CHILLIES

Peppers and chillies can be pickled in vinegar. This quantity will fill a medium-sized jar with whole chillies, preserved with herbs and garlic and up to 675ml/1½ pints/3 cups of vinegar. Increase the vinegar quantity and dilute it with a little water if you want to preserve a larger quantity of chillies, or sweet red and yellow peppers, which should first have their caps, seeds and pithy membranes removed.

225g/8oz whole fresh chillies
350ml/12fl oz/1½ cups white wine vinegar
1 tsp salt
sprig of bay
sprig of rosemary
4 cloves of garlic, peeled
up to 350ml/12fl oz/1½ cups
extra white wine vinegar

Inspect the chillies for damage, discarding any that are bruised, lacerated or otherwise blemished. Snip off all but the base of their stems. Bring the vinegar and the chillies to a boil in a pan. Add the remaining ingredients except the vinegar and simmer for 6–8 minutes. With a clean spoon, transfer them to a jar previously sterilized with freshly boiled water. Pour in the pickling liquid with its herbs, top up with the additional vinegar to cover, and allow to cool before sealing. The chillies will be ready within a month.

GIN PEPPERS

This is a family recipe for the tiny wild chillies that grew on little bushes in our tropical garden in Port of Spain, the capital of Trinidad and Tobago. Use the hottest fresh chillies available, or substitute small, dried red chillies, chopped or crumbled. The gin peppers should last almost indefinitely if topped up occasionally with fresh booze and additional chillies.

Fill a clean small bottle with gin or sherry. Finely slice a handful of very hot fresh chillies and put them in the bottle, seeds and all. Fill the bottle with gin, screw on the lid, or stop with a cork, and leave to infuse for about a month before using very sparingly as a seasoning for hot Oriental or Mexican dishes, as required.

CHILLI OIL

Chilli oil can be bought already bottled in Oriental stores. However, it is easy and inexpensive to make your own lethal concoction to spike Chinese stir-fries and soups, as follows:

Lightly toast 2 tsp of lightly crushed Szechuan peppercorns (or black peppercorns) in a hot, dry pan. Put them into a clean, glass bottle that holds about 140ml/5fl oz of liquid. Add 1 tbs of very hot dried red chillies that you have crushed, seeds and all, with a mortar and pestle or in a coffee grinder. Fill up with peanut or other vegetable oil, stirring well with the blade of a knife to release any air pockets, and to allow the oil to penetrate the deposit of peppers thoroughly. Screw on the lid or stop with a cork, and let the oil steep in the peppers for a month or more. Strain the oil into a fresh little bottle and use sparingly.